Dad's Surprise

GW01553238

One Lady of Mercy, N.S.
BANTRY,
Co. CORK.

Written by Tracey Reeder   Illustrated by Jiri Tibor Novak

The grass was getting long.
"When are you going to cut the grass?"
Mum asked.

"I have some shopping to do this morning.
I'll do it after that," Dad said.

Dad was gone for a long time.
When he got home he called out,
"Come and see my surprise."

We all ran outside.
It was as big as a go-kart
but it wasn't a go-kart.

3

It was as red as a fire engine
but it wasn't a fire engine.

Dad said, "It has to be that colour,
so people can see it."

It had four black wheels,
just like a car.
But it wasn't a car.

Dad said, "The wheels have to be
tough, so you can work in the rain."

It had two bright lights at the front,
just like a train.
But it wasn't a train.

Dad said, "The lights have to be strong,
so you can work at night."

It had a big blade,
just like a knife.
But it wasn't a knife.

Dad said,
"The blade has to be sharp,
to cut through everything."

Dad hopped on.
He started the engine,
and off he drove
on his new mower.

"At last," said Mum.
"The grass is getting cut."